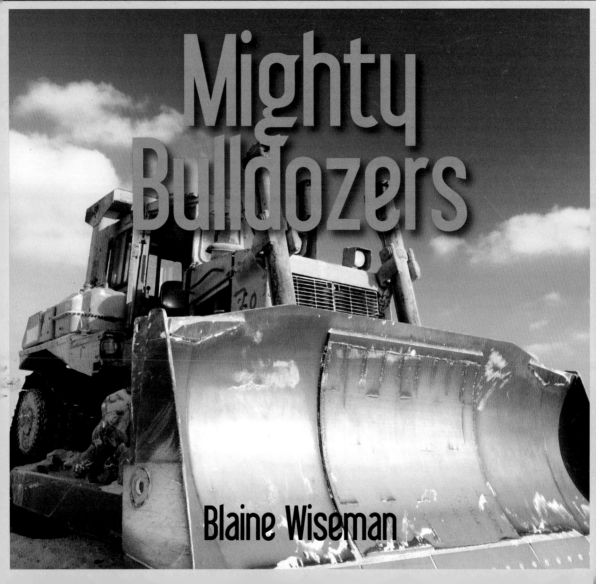

Mighty
Bulldozers

Blaine Wiseman

Published by Weigl Publishers Inc.
350 5th Avenue, 59th Floor
New York, NY 10118
Website: www.weigl.com

Library of Congress Cataloging-in-Publication Data

Wiseman, Blaine.
 Bulldozers : WOW big machines / Blaine Wiseman.
     p. cm.
 Includes index.
 ISBN 978-1-61690-142-4 (hardcover : alk. paper) -- ISBN 978-1-61690-143-1 (softcover : alk. paper) -- ISBN 978-1-61690-144-8 (e-book)
1. Bulldozers--Juvenile literature. I. Title.
 TA735.W567 2011
 624.1'52--dc22
                                    2010013933

Printed in the United States of America in North Mankato, Minnesota
2 3 4 5 6 7 8 9 0 15 14 13 12 11

022011
WEP040211

Editor: Heather C. Hudak
Design: Terry Paulhus

Weigl acknowledges Getty Images as its primary image supplier for this title.

CONTENTS

What are Bulldozers?

Have you ever wondered how construction workers move huge piles of dirt and tear down buildings? They use big machines, such as bulldozers. A bulldozer can be used to fill holes, flatten ground, or move heavy objects.

Bulldozers have a large blade on the front. The blade pushes dirt from place to place. Some bulldozers have a hook on the back. The hook is used to rip up the ground.

Bulldozers are named after bulls. Like bulls, bulldozers are very strong.

Big Bulls

How big is your family car? The average car weighs about 4,000 pounds (1,814 kilograms). Even the smallest bulldozers weigh twice as much as a car.

The world's biggest bulldozer weighs more than 22 elephants. It is 16 feet (4.9 meters) tall, 41 feet (12.5 m) long, and 24 feet (7.3 m) wide. This big machine has enough power to move 485,000 pounds (219,992 kg) at one time.

Moving Materials

Did you know that a bulldozer can move 20,000 pounds (9,072 kg) in seconds? It would take about 200 people to push the same amount of rock by hand.

Bulldozers can move almost any object. They can rip apart mountains and push rocks and dirt to a new place. The huge blade on the front of a bulldozer pushes dirt, rocks, trees, and other objects.

9

Making Tracks

Why are some bulldozers called crawlers or caterpillars? These bulldozers have tracks instead of wheels. The tracks make the bulldozer look like a caterpillar crawling along the ground.

Tracks keep bulldozers from sinking on wet, muddy, or sandy ground. They move more easily than wheels across uneven ground. Bulldozers on tracks need less space to turn. This makes working in tight spaces easier.

Rip It Up

Have you ever used your fingers like a hook to dig in mud or sand? The hook on a bulldozer is called a ripper. It is a powerful claw. It digs into the ground and tears it apart.

Bulldozers can have many rippers that are side-by-side on the back of the machine. Work can be done faster if more than one ripper is used.

Some rippers are so strong that they can break through hardened **lava**.

Bull Blades

Did you know that bulldozers have more than one type of blade? Bulldozers have three main types of blades. Each does a different job.

The straight blade is short and flat. It is used to loosen and level dirt. The second type of blade is tall and curved. It has side wings to keep objects in place. This type of blade is used to gather and move materials. A third type of blade is used to push rocks and other objects. It has smaller sides and is less curved than the other types of blades.

Army Armor

How can bulldozers be used to help soldiers? Trash, damaged cars, or other items sometimes block roads where soldiers work. Bulldozers that are covered in armor push these items out of the way. They also protect soldiers from bullets, **land mines**, and **grenades**.

Bull Rider

How do drivers move the giant parts of a bulldozer? The driver controls the bulldozer using levers. One lever changes the direction and speed of the bulldozer. A second lever moves the blade up and down.

A special system is used to power the blade and the ripper. This system makes large amounts of energy by squeezing oil from one tube to another. This creates power in a part of the bulldozer that had none before. Oil flows into a tube when a lever is pushed. This makes the blade or ripper move.

19

Bringing Down the House

Have you ever seen a house being torn down? Sometimes, people want to tear down an old house to build a new one on the land. A bulldozer can knock down the old house in just a few minutes. Then, the machine can be used to clear the pieces away.

Bulldozers also can be used to move around waste. At **landfills**, bulldozers push garbage into holes. Then, these big machines cover the holes with dirt.

Build a Bulldozer

Supplies

tape, scissors, ruler, pipe cleaner, colored pencils or crayons, three toilet paper tubes, glue, black and yellow construction paper, and a small, rectangular box

1. With the help of an adult, measure each side of the box with the ruler. Cut the yellow construction paper to size.

2. Glue the yellow construction paper to each side of the box. Make sure the box is completely covered. The yellow box will be the main part of the bulldozer's body.

3. Using the colored pencils or crayons, draw windows, doors, lights, and other designs on the outside of the box.

4. Cut the toilet paper tube in half lengthwise, and spread it apart. This is the bulldozer blade.

5. Bend the pipe cleaner, and tape it to the back of the toilet paper tube.

6. Tape the two ends of the pipe cleaner to the front of the bulldozer.

7. Cut two pieces of black construction paper twice as long as the bulldozer.

8. Fold one piece of construction paper in half, and tape the two ends together. This is one of the tracks. Do the same with the other piece of black construction paper.

9. Tape the tracks to each side of the bulldozer. Place a toilet paper tube inside each track to hold it open.

10. Have fun using the bulldozer to push around blocks and toys.

Find Out More

To learn more about bulldozers, visit these websites.

Bulldozer Video
http://video.yahoo.com/watch/772344/3300420

Great Bulldozer
www.squidoo.com/bulldozers

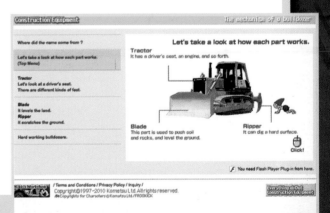

Everything About Construction
www.kenkenkikki.jp/special/no02/e_index.htm

Glossary

grenades: explosive devices

landfills: places where people in a city or town take their trash

land mines: bombs that are planted in the ground and explode when weight is applied to them

lava: hot liquid rock that flows from a volcano

Index